The Battle of Seven Pines: The History of the First Major Battle of the 1862 Peninsula Campaign

By Charles River Editors

A depiction of the battle

About Charles River Editors

Charles River Editors provides superior editing and original writing services in the digital publishing industry, with the expertise to create digital content for publishers across a vast range of subject matter. In addition to providing original digital content for third party publishers, we also republish civilization's greatest literary works, bringing them to new generations of readers via ebooks.

Sign up here to receive updates about free books as we publish them, and visit Our Kindle Author Page to browse today's free promotions and our most recently published Kindle titles.

Introduction

A contemporary depiction of the battle

The Battle of Seven Pines

As Union commander George McClellan moved the Army of the Potomac up the Peninsula in early 1862, the Union army still had a nearly 2-1 advantage in manpower, so Army of Northern Virginia commander Joseph E. Johnston continued to gradually pull his troops back to a line of defense nearer Richmond as McClellan advanced. In conjunction, the Union Navy began moving its operations further up the James River, until it could get within 7 miles of the Confederate capital before being opposed by a Southern fort.

McClellan continued to attempt to turn Johnston's flank, until the two armies were facing each other along the Chickahominy River. At this point, the Union army was close enough to Richmond that they could see the city's church steeples, but they would come no closer. By the end of May, Stonewall Jackson had startlingly defeated three separate Northern armies in the Valley, inducing Lincoln to hold back the I Corps from McClellan. When McClellan was forced to extend his line north to link up with troops that he expected to be sent overland to him, Johnston learned that McClellan was moving along the Chickahominy River.

It was at this point that Johnston got uncharacteristically aggressive. Johnston had run out of breathing space for his army, and he believed McClellan was seeking to link up with

McDowell's forces. Moreover, about a third of McClellan's army was south of the river, while the other parts of the army were still north of it, offering Johnston an enticing target. After a quick deluge turned the river into a rushing torrent that would make it impossible or the Union army to link back up or aid each other, Johnston drew up a very complex plan of attack for different wings of his army, and struck at the Army of the Potomac at the Battle of Seven Pines on May 31, 1862.

Like Union general Irvin McDowell's plan for First Bull Run, the plan proved too complicated for Johnston's army to execute, and after a day of bloody fighting little was accomplished from a technical standpoint. At one point during the Battle of Seven Pines, Confederates under General James Longstreet marched in the wrong direction down the wrong road, causing congestion and confusion among other Confederate units and ultimately weakening the effectiveness of the massive Confederate counterattack launched against McClellan. Johnston wrote in his memoirs, "The operations of the Confederate troops in this battle were very much retarded by the dense woods and thickets that covered the ground, and by the deep mud and broad ponds of rain-water, in many places more than knee-deep, through which they had to struggle."

Nonetheless, by the time the fighting was finished, nearly 40,000 had been engaged on both sides, and it was the biggest battle in the Eastern theater to date (second only to Shiloh at the time). Although it was inconclusive, McClellan was rattled by the attack, and near the end of the fighting that night Johnston had attempted to rally his men by riding up and down the lines only to be nearly blown off his horse by artillery fire and having to be taken off the field. Johnston explained, "About seven o'clock I received a slight wound in the right shoulder from a musket-shot, and, a few moments after, was unhorsed by a heavy fragment of shell which struck my breast. Those around had me borne from the field in an ambulance; not, however, before the President, who was with General Lee, not far in the rear, had heard of the accident, and visited me, manifesting great concern, as he continued to do until I was out of danger." Having been seriously wounded, Johnston's command was given the following day to military advisor Robert E. Lee.

The Battle of Seven Pines: The History of the First Major Battle of the 1862 Peninsula Campaign looks at the events that led to one of the most fateful battles of the Civil War. Along with pictures of important people, places, and events, you will learn about the Battle of Seven Pines like never before, in no time at all.

The Battle of Seven Pines: The History of the First Major Battle of the 1862 Peninsula Campaign

Chapter 1: Preparing the Peninsula Campaign

After First Manassas, the Confederate army under General Joseph E. Johnston stayed camped near the outskirts of Washington D.C., while the North reorganized the Army of the Potomac under Johnston's acquaintance, George B. McClellan. McClellan was widely considered a prodigy thanks to his West Point years, his service in Mexico, his observation during the Crimean War, and his oft-forgotten campaign in Western Virginia against Robert E. Lee in 1861. Though he is best known for his shortcomings today, McClellan had nearly ended Lee's Civil War career before it started, as General Lee was blamed throughout the South for losing western Virginia after his defeat at the Battle of Cheat Mountain. Lee would eventually be reassigned to constructing coastal defenses on the East Coast, and when his men dug trenches in preparation for the defense of Richmond, he was derisively dubbed the "King of Spades". That Lee was even in position to assume command of the Army of Northern Virginia the following year during the Peninsula Campaign was due more to his friendship with Jefferson Davis than anything else.

McClellan

Johnston

During the Civil War, one of the tales that was often told among Confederate soldiers was that Joseph E. Johnston was a crack shot who was a better bird hunter than just about everyone else in the South. However, as the story went, Johnston would never take the shot when asked to, complaining that something was wrong with the situation that prevented him from being able to shoot the bird when it was time. The story is almost certainly apocryphal, used to demonstrate the Confederates' frustration with a man who everyone regarded as a capable general. Johnston began the Civil War as one of the senior commanders, leading (ironically) the Army of the Potomac to victory in the Battle of First Bull Run over Irvin McDowell's Union Army. But Johnston would become known more for losing by not winning. Johnston was never badly beaten in battle, but he had a habit of "strategically withdrawing" until he had nowhere else to go.

Meanwhile, as he was reorganizing the Army of the Potomac, McClellan vastly overestimated the strength of Johnston's army, leading him to plan an amphibious assault on Richmond that avoided Johnston's army in his front. In response, Johnston moved his army toward Culpeper Court House, which angered President Davis because it signified a retreat. For that reason, Davis brought Lee to Richmond as a military adviser, and he began to constrain Johnston's authority by issuing direct orders himself.

Despite Confederate misgivings, Johnston's movement had disrupted McClellan's anticipated landing spot, and McClellan had already faced a number of issues in planning the campaign even before reaching the jump-off point. The first option for the landing spot (Urbana) had been scrapped, and there was bickering over the amount of troops left around Washington without the Army of the Potomac fighting on the Overland line. Moreover, McClellan had to deal with politics; the Joint Committee on the Conduct of the War (which included Senators Wade, Chandler, and Johnson, the future Vice President grew increasingly leery of his intentions and insisted on knowing why, after five months of intense training, McClellan's troops had still not engaged the enemy. "General," Wade stated, "you have all the troops you have called for, and if you haven't enough, you shall have more. They are well organized and equipped, and the loyal people of this country expect that you will make a short and decisive campaign. To this McClellan responded haughtily that "we must bear in mind the necessity of having everything ready in case of a defeat…" Dismissing McClellan, Chandler turned to Wade and scoffed, "I don't know much about war, but it seems to me that this is infernal, unmitigated cowardice!"

The Joint Committee began demanding that Lincoln replace the problematic McClellan, fearing that McClellan's impotence would lead to the capture of Washington. Increasingly disturbed by his new commanding officer's indolence (and receiving unrelenting pressure from Secretary of War Edwin W. Stanton and the Joint Committee), on January 27, 1862, Lincoln issued his famed General War Order No. 1, which called for the forward movement of all Union armies by February 22, 1862 (a move in part intended to derail any reluctance from other field generals who may attempt to pull similar delay strategies). Undeterred, McClellan was able to convince Lincoln to postpone the order for two months to allow his men to better prepare. He then persuaded Lincoln to change his strategy for the planned offensive against Richmond, convincing him that the attack would be more effective if launched from the peninsula between the York and James rivers rather than by the proposed Overland north-south route. Ultimately, McClellan would abandon this plan before launching the Peninsula Campaign at a different landing.

On March 8, Lincoln, nearly at the end of his patience, sought to appease McClellan, the Joint Committee, and his twelve division commanders by allowing McClellan to present his proposed

"Urbanna Plan" for military evaluation. To Lincoln's surprise, the plan was accepted by a vote of eight to four, thus leaving him no choice but do what was possible to push the plan forward. Following the Committee's recommendation to break the Army of the Potomac into individually-commanded corps, each headed by a specially-chosen corps commander, Lincoln called for McClellan to select corps leaders. McClellan, however, balked at the idea, citing that he did not yet know his men well enough to know their strengths and weaknesses. Feeling he was left with no choice, Lincoln issued General War Order No. 2, appointing McDowell, Edwin "Bull" Sumner, S. P. Heintzelman, and E. D. Keyes to corps command, effective immediately. To McClellan's dismay, and fuelling his belief that his superiors wanted him to fail, three of those appointed had opposed the plan.

Heintzelman

Sumner

Keyes

Later that same day, Lincoln sent word for McClellan to meet with him after breakfast. At that meeting, Lincoln reluctantly repeated rumors of charges that were circulating among his staff; charges that touched his honor as a soldier. Lincoln said reluctantly, "There is a very ugly matter . . . a rumor that the Urbanna Plan was conceived with the traitorous intent of removing its defenders from Washington, and thus giving over to the enemy the capital and government, thus left defenseless." Incensed, McClellan stood and stated emphatically, "I will permit no one to couple the word treason with my name!" Apologizing, Lincoln let the matter go at that, dismissing McClellan. A short time later, however, McClellan returned to the President's office with his twelve division commanders in tow to compel them to voice their support of his plan in front of the President. By this point, McClellan had resigned himself to having to outmaneuver Lincoln when need be.

Three days later, on March 11, 1862, McClellan received word that President Lincoln had issued another War Order (No. 3), relieving him as General-in-Chief but allowing him to retain his position as commander of the Army of the Potomac, the biggest of seven armies in the

Eastern theater. With time passing and the pieces of McClellan's Urbanna Plan now falling apart, Lincoln had done what he had to do to maintain order.

Finally, in March 1862, after nine months in command, General McClellan began his invasion of Virginia, initiating what would become known as the Peninsula Campaign. Showing his proclivity for turning movement and grand strategy, McClellan completely shifted the theater of operations; rather than march directly into Richmond and use his superior numbers to assert domination, he opted to exploit the Union naval dominance and move his army via an immense naval flotilla down the Potomac into Chesapeake Bay and land at Fort Monroe in Hampton, Virginia, at the southern tip of the Virginia Peninsula. In addition to his 130,000 thousand men, he moved 15,000 thousand horses and mules by boat as well. There he planned for an additional 80,000 men to join him, at which time he would advance westward to Richmond. One of the European observers likened the launch of the campaign to the "stride of a giant."

Chapter 2: Moving Towards Richmond

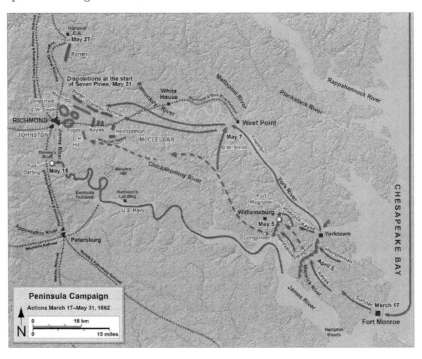

A map or the armies' marches towards Richmond

McClellan's Peninsula Campaign has been analyzed meticulously and is considered one of the grandest failures of the Union war effort, with McClellan made the scapegoat. In actuality, there was plenty of blame to go around, including Lincoln and his Administration, which was so concerned about Stonewall Jackson's army in the Shenandoah Valley that several Union armies were left in the Valley to defend Washington D.C., and even more were held back from McClellan for fear of the capital's safety. The Administration also micromanaged the deployment of certain divisions, and with Stanton's decision to shut down recruiting stations in early 1862, combined with the Confederacy concentrating all their troops in the area, the Army of the Potomac was eventually outnumbered in front of Richmond.

At the beginning of the campaign, however, McClellan had vastly superior numbers at his disposal, with only about 70,000 Confederate troops on the entirety of the peninsula and fewer than 17,000 between him and Richmond. McClellan was unaware of this decisive advantage, however, because of the intelligence reports he kept receiving from Allen Pinkerton, which vastly overstated the number of available Confederate soldiers.

As Johnston marched his army to oppose McClellan, he was fully aware that he was severely outnumbered, even if McClellan didn't know that. For that reason, he was in constant communication with the leadership in Richmond, and in April he continued trying to persuade Davis and Lee that the best course of action would be to dig in and fight defensively around Richmond. President Davis would have none of it.

From the beginning, McClellan's caution and the narrow width of the Peninsula worked against his army. At Yorktown, which had been the site of a decisive siege during the Revolution, McClellan's initial hopes of surrounding and enveloping the Confederate lines through the use of the Navy was scuttled when the Navy couldn't promise that it'd be able to operate in the area. That allowed General John Magruder, whose Confederate forces were outmanned nearly 4-1, to hold Yorktown for the entire month of April. Magruder accomplished it by completely deceiving the federals, at times marching his men in circles to make McClellan think his army was many times larger. Other times, he spread his artillery batteries across the line and fired liberally and sporadically at the Union lines, just to give the impression that the Confederates had huge numbers. The ruse worked, leaving the Union command thinking there were 100,000 Confederates.

Magruder

As a result of the misimpressions, McClellan chose not to attack Yorktown in force, instead opting to lay siege to it. In part, this was due to the decisive advantage the Union had in siege equipment, including massive mortars and artillery. The siege successfully captured Yorktown in early May with only about 500 casualties, but Magruder bought enough time for Johnston to march south and confront McClellan on the Peninsula.

After taking Yorktown, McClellan sent George Stoneman's cavalry in pursuit and attempted to move swiftly enough to cut off Johnston's retreat by use of Navy ships. At the battle of Williamsburg, which the Confederates fought as a delaying action to retreat, Winfield Scott Hancock led his brigade in a successful flanking attack against General Longstreet's Confederates and quickly occupied two abandoned Confederate strongholds. Hancock's brigade then sharply repulsed a Confederate assault by the 24th Virginia regiment.

At this point, Hancock had been ordered by General Edwin "Bull" Sumner to pull back his men to Cub Creek, but he instead decided to hold his ground, and his men repulsed an assault by the 5th North Carolina regiment in short order. As Confederate General D.H. Hill scrambled to stop that regiment's assault, Hancock's men counterattacked and drove them off the field, inflicting nearly 1,000 casualties on the two regiments that had attacked his brigade and losing just 100.

The Battle of Williamsburg was ultimately inconclusive, with the Confederates suffering 1600 casualties and the Army of the Potomac suffering 2200, but McClellan labeled it a "brilliant victory" over superior forces. While that was inaccurate, the press accounts of Hancock's performance fairly earned him national renown, and McClellan telegraphed Washington to report, "Hancock was superb today." Hancock had just won the nickname "Hancock the Superb."

Hancock

Chapter 3: Planning for Battle

As Johnston pulled back, he decided to have his army dig in with the Chickahominy River in front of it, which he could use as a natural barrier. Meanwhile, McClellan stretched his line further to the northeast so that McDowell's I Corps, which was supposed to march south and join the Army of the Potomac, would have its transportation lines covered by Union forces. Once his men were in position, McClellan began to have his army dig in to make it almost unassailable.

In fact, McDowell's corps was not on the way to McClellan, but Johnston believed he was and changed the Confederate dispositions to attack McClellan before McDowell arrived. Confederate general James Longstreet explained in his memoirs, "On the 27th, General Johnston received information that General McDowell's corps was at Fredericksburg, and on the march to reinforce McClellan's right at Mechanicsville. He prepared to attack McClellan before McDowell could reach him. To this end he withdrew Smith's division from the Williamsburg road, relieving it by the division of D. H. Hill; withdrew Longstreet's division from its position, and A. P. Hill's from

Ashland. The fighting column was to be under General G. W. Smith, his next in rank, and General Whiting was assigned command of Smith's division,--the column to consist of A. P. Hill's, Whiting's, and D. R. Jones's divisions. The latter was posted between the Mechanicsville pike and Meadow Bridge road. A. P. Hill was to march direct against McClellan's outpost at Mechanicsville, Whiting to cross the river at Meadow Bridge, and D. R. Jones at Mechanicsville, thus completing the column of attack on the east side. I was to march by the Mechanicsville road to the vicinity of the bridge, and to strike down against the Federal right, west of the river, the march to be made during the night; D. H. Hill to post a brigade on his right on the Charles City road to guard the field to be left by his division, as well as the line left vacant by Longstreet's division."

Longstreet

In reality, Washington had become so skittish about Stonewall Jackson's actions in the Shenandoah Valley, where the Confederate general had confounded three different Union armies, that the administration ultimately ordered McDowell to the Valley. This was almost certainly unnecessary in the first place, and it was even more pointless when Jackson's army left the Valley in June to link up with the Army of Northern Virginia outside Richmond.

On the 27th, the Confederates learned that McDowell was not marching south, but many of the generals still believed an attack was prudent, and that the Confederates couldn't win a siege. Longstreet explained, "At nightfall the troops took up the march for their several assigned positions. Before dark General Johnston called a number of his officers together for instructions,--viz., Smith, Magruder, Stuart, and Longstreet. When we were assembled, General Johnston announced later information: that McDowell's line of march had been changed,--that he was going north. Following the report of this information, General Smith proposed that the plan for battle should be given up, in view of the very strong ground at Beaver Dam Creek.1 I urged that the plan laid against the concentrating columns was made stronger by the change of direction of McDowell's column, and should suggest more prompt and vigorous prosecution. In this Magruder and Stuart joined me. The pros and cons were talked over till a late hour, when at last General Johnston, weary of it, walked aside to a separate seat. I took the opportunity to draw near him, and suggested that the Federal position behind Beaver Dam Creek, so seriously objected to by General Smith, could be turned by marching to and along the high ground between the Chickahominy and Pamunkey Rivers; that the position of the enemy when turned would be abandoned without a severe struggle, and give a fair field for battle; that we should not lose the opportunity to await another possible one."

The most notable aspect of the Union line in the Confederates' opinion was that it had a concave shape, and as a result, the Army of the Potomac's left flank was not on the same side of the Chickahominy as the rest of the army. Thus, if the Confederates could successfully attack the Union left on its side of the river, they would be isolated from help and could possibly be destroyed in detail. In his memoirs, Johnston explained:

"Longstreet, as ranking officer of the three divisions to be united near Hill's camp, was instructed, verbally, to form his own and Hill's division in two lines crossing the Williamsburg road at right angles, and to advance to the attack in that order; while Huger's division should march along the Charles City road by the right flank, to fall upon the enemy's left flank as soon as our troops became engaged with them in front. It was understood that abatis, or earthworks, that might be encountered, should be turned. General Smith was to engage any troops that might cross the Chickahominy to assist Heintzelman's and Keyes's corps; or, if none came, he was to fall upon the right flanks of those troops engaged with Longstreet. The accident of location prevented the assignment of this officer to the command of the principal attack, to which he was entitled by his rank. As his division was on the left of all those to be engaged, it was apprehended that its transfer to the right might cause a serious loss of time.

"The rain began to fall violently in the afternoon, and continued all night; and, in the morning, the little streams near our camps were so much swollen as to make it seem probable that the Chickahominy was overflowing its banks, and cutting the communication between the two parts of the Federal army.

"Being confident that Longstreet and Hill, with their forces united, would be successful in the earlier part of the action against an enemy formed in several lines, with wide intervals between them, I left the immediate control, on the Williamsburg road, to them, under general instructions, and placed myself on the left, where I could soonest learn the approach of Federal reenforcements from beyond the Chickahominy. From this point scouts and reconnoitering parties were sent forward to detect such movements, should they be made."

Longstreet was also confident in the plan's success, as he noted in his memoirs:

"The plan settled upon was that the attack should be made by General D. H. Hill's division on the Williamsburg road, supported by Longstreet's division. Huger's division, just out of garrison duty at Norfolk, was to march between Hill's right and the swamp against the enemy's line of skirmishers, and move abreast of the battle; G. W. Smith's division, under Whiting, to march by the Gaines road to Old Tavern, and move abreast of the battle on its left. The field before Old Tavern was not carefully covered by the enemy's skirmishers north of Fair Oaks, nor by parties in observation.

"Experience during the discussion of the battle ordered for the 28th caused me to doubt of effective work from the troops ordered for the left flank, but the plan seemed so simple that it was thought impossible for any one to go dangerously wrong; and General Johnston stated that he would be on that road, the better to receive from his troops along the crest of the Chickahominy information of movements of the enemy on the farther side of the river, and to look to the co-operation of the troops on the Nine Miles road.

To facilitate marches, Huger's division was to have the Charles City road to the head of White Oak Swamp, file across it and march down its northern margin; D. H. Hill to have the Williamsburg road to the enemy's front; Longstreet's division to march by the Nine Miles road and a lateral road leading across the rear of General Hill on the Williamsburg road; G. W. Smith by the Gaines road to Old Tavern on the Nine Miles road."

Longstreet wrote that he didn't think it was possible to suffer a serious hitch in the plans, but the planning required coordination among numerous Confederate divisions on multiple roads, which could only make timing a problem. As the events of May 31 would prove, things would go awry from the beginning.

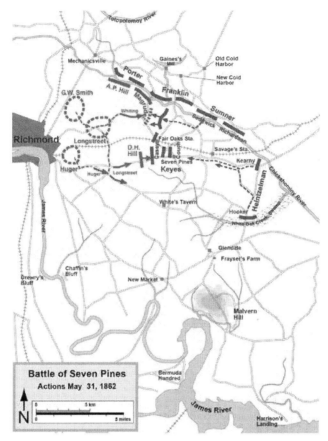

A map of the lines on May 31

Johnston intended for the Confederate attack to start as early as possible on May 31, but those wishes would never come close to fruition. Part of this was due to the vague orders he gave his division commander Huger, which failed to fix a time for attack:

> "The reports of Major-General D. H. Hill give me the impression that the enemy is in considerable strength in his front. It seems to me necessary that we should increase our force also; for that object I wish to concentrate the troops of your division on the Charles City road, and to concentrate the troops of Major-General

Hill on the Williamsburg road. To do this it will be necessary for you to move, as early in the morning as possible, to relieve the brigade of General Hill's division now on the Charles City road. I have desired General Hill to send you a guide. The road is the second large one diverging to the right from the Williamsburg road. The first turns off near the tollgate. On reaching your position on the Charles City road, learn at once the route to the main roads, to Richmond on your right and left, especially those to the left, and try to find guides. Be ready, if an action should begin on your left, to fall upon the enemy's left flank.

"Most respectfully your obedient servant, J. E. Johnston.

P. S.--It is necessary to move very early."

Huger

Due to those orders, Huger had no idea what was going on during the early morning until another Confederate division was passing by his own on the road. Moreover, from the beginning of the day, the use of different roads confounded various Confederate generals, and the problems were exacerbated by flooding in the area as a result of heavy rainfall over the previous few days. Longstreet explained some of the early trouble: "Subsequent events seem to call for mention just here that General Smith, instead of moving the troops by the route assigned them, marched back to the Nine Miles road near the city, rode to Johnston's Headquarters about six in the morning, and reported that he was with the division, but not for the purpose of taking command from General Whiting. As General Johnston did not care to order him back to his position as commander of the left wing, he set himself to work to make trouble, complained that my troops were on the Nine Miles road in the way of his march, and presently complained that they had left that road and were over on the Williamsburg road, and induced General Johnston to so far modify the plans as to order three of my brigades down the Nine Miles road to the New Bridge fork."

Unfortunately for the Confederates, those orders wouldn't reach the front because the courier rode into Union lines and was captured before reporting the information. While this compelled the Union generals to (mistakenly) think the attack would come down the Nine Miles Road, it caused severe congestion and mix-ups among the Confederates on the right side of their line.

Even at this point, with confusion about orders and roads, and flooding delaying movements, Longstreet believed by 9:00 a.m. that the marches and dispositions could be straightened out enough to deliver an overwhelming attack on the Union left: "My march by the Nine Miles and lateral roads leading across to the Williamsburg road was interrupted by the flooded grounds about the head of Gillis Creek. At the same time this creek was bank full, where it found a channel for its flow into the James. The delay of an hour to construct a bridge was preferred to the encounter of more serious obstacles along the narrow lateral road, flooded by the storm. As we were earlier at the creek, it gave us precedence over Huger's division, which had to cross after us. The division was prepared with cooked rations, had wagons packed at six o'clock, and rested in the rear of General Hill's at nine A. M. Meanwhile, General G. W. Smith's division had marched by the Nine Miles road and was resting near the fork of the New Bridge road at Old Tavern. Upon meeting General Huger in the morning, I gave him a succinct account of General Johnston's plans and wishes; after which he inquired as to the dates of our commissions, which revealed that he was the ranking officer, when I suggested that it was only necessary for him to take command and execute the orders. This he declined. Then it was proposed that he should send two of his brigades across to join on the right of the column of attack, while he could remain with his other brigade, which was to relieve that of General Hill on the Charles City road. Though he expressed himself satisfied with this, his manner was eloquent of discontent. The better to harmonize, I proposed to reinforce his column by three of my brigades, to be sent under

General Wilcox, to lead or follow his division, as he might order. Under this arrangement it seemed that concert of action was assured. I gave especial orders to General Wilcox to have care that the head of his column was abreast the battle when it opened, and rode forward to join General Hill, my other three brigades advancing along the Williamsburg road."

Smith

While the Confederates were moving along the roads, the Union was able to see the marches thanks to the efforts of Thaddeus Lowe's observation balloon. Around noon, Lowe was hovering above the area and was able to relay news of Confederate battle formations back to the Union headquarters. Unfortunately for the Army of the Potomac, McClellan was ill, but news of an imminent Confederate attack made its way around camp in the early afternoon, several hours after Johnston had hoped to begin the assault.

A picture of Lowe using an observation balloon at Seven Pines

As it turned out, the fighting began around 1:00 p.m. mostly because Confederate division commander D.H. Hill, one of the South's most competent generals, was tired of the delays. Hill's division was to be the vanguard of the attack, and since his men were in the front, they had avoided some of the confusion on the roads behind them and were thus in position by early morning. Hill bristled as he waited for men from Longstreet and Huger's commands, and eventually, he decided to fire off a signal gun around noon. With that, the time for an attack by his division was set for about 1:00 p.m., about five hours after Johnston had originally planned, and as fate would have it, acoustics in the area prevented Johnston from hearing the signal gun and being aware of his own army's attack. Indeed, Johnston would not learn of the ongoing engagement until about 4:00 p.m. that day, and he incorrectly asserted in his memoirs that the Confederate assault started around 3:00.

When Hill started the attack around 1:00 p.m. that day, he was hurling four brigades against Silas Casey's Union division in his front, and even though Hill's men accounted for less than $1/3^{rd}$ of the anticipated attacking force, his men immediately began to push the inexperienced federals back. At this early moment in the battle, Hill was still waiting for Huger's men to join the attack, and he eventually got so tired of waiting that he decided to try to turn the Union flank with just one of his own brigades. Longstreet discussed the early part of the action by Hill's division: "He had four brigades, and was ordered to advance in columns of brigades, two on each side of the road. Garland's and G. B. Anderson's brigades in columns, preceded by skirmishers, advanced on the left of the road at the sound of the guns, and engaged after a short march from the starting. As Rodes's brigade was not yet in position, some little time elapsed before the columns on the right moved, so that Garland's column encountered more than its share of early fight, but Rodes, supported by Rains's brigade, came promptly to his relief, which steadied the advance. The enemy's front was reinforced and arrested progress of our skirmishers, but a way was found by which the enemy was turned out of position, and by and by the open before the intrenched camp was reached."

Casey

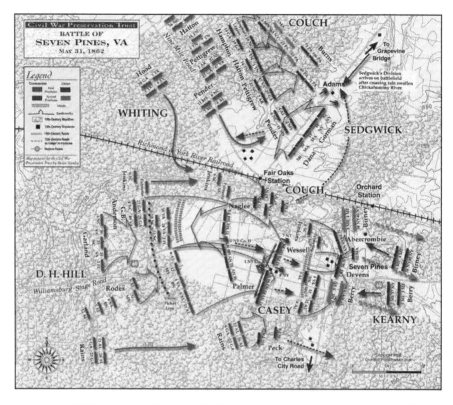

A map of Hill's attack on Casey and the Union reinforcements arriving under Phil Kearny

As Casey's men found themselves suddenly in a desperate fight for control of their fortifications, the division commander sent word back to his corps commander Keyes that he needed reinforcements. For unknown reasons, Keyes was slow to respond, and all the while, McClellan remained bedridden and generally unaware of the danger posed to his army's left flank. Even as late as 2:30, nearly 90 minutes after the fighting had started, Union headquarters remained in the dark about the situation across the Chickahominy.

As Casey's division fell back to a second line of defenses, they were bolstered by Couch's division in Keyes' IV Corps, but this coincided with Hill finally receiving reinforcements from behind him. This led to savage fighting across the second line of defenses by the middle of the afternoon, as Longstreet explained, "The battle moved bravely on. R. H. Anderson's brigade was ordered to support its left at Fair Oaks, and Pickett's, on the railroad, was drawn near. Hill met

Casey's troops rallying, and reinforcements with them coming to recover the lost ground, but they were forced back to the second intrenched line (Couch's), where severe fighting ensued, but the line was carried at two o'clock, cutting Couch with four regiments and two companies of infantry, and Brady's six-gun battery, off at Fair Oaks Station. Finding that he could not cut his way back to his command, Couch stood back from the railroad and presently opened his battery fire across our advancing lines. As he was standing directly in front of Smith's division, we thought that he would soon be attacked and driven off. Nevertheless, it was not prudent to leave that point on our flank unguarded until we found Smith's division in action. The force was shut off from our view by the thick pine wood, so that we could know nothing of its strength, and only knew of its position from its artillery fire. We could not attack it lest we should fall under the fire of the division in position for that attack. Anderson's other regiments, under the gallant Colonel M. Jenkins, were ordered into Hill's forward battle, as his troops were worn. Jenkins soon found himself in the van, and so swiftly led on that the discomfited troops found no opportunity to rally. Reinforcements from the Third Corps came, but in the swampy wood Jenkins was prompt enough to strike their heads as their retreating comrades passed. Right and left and front he applied his beautiful tactics and pushed his battle. "

With the fighting becoming more severe, commanders on both sides could hear the noise of the battle, but the wooded nature of the terrain often concealed views of what was going on, and in the case of the Army of the Potomac, most of the soldiers were across a river that had been swollen by rain. While Phil Kearny's division from Heintzelman's III Corps was able to easily march to the battle because they were south of the river, any other potential Union reinforcements would have to cross the river, a logistical feat made more difficult by the rushing torrents and the fact most of the bridges in the area had been destroyed by the retreating Confederates earlier.

Kearny

On the other side, Johnston finally learned of Hill's initial assault due to communications from Longstreet, but he only learned about it right around the time Hill was preparing to assault the second line of defense, which consisted of Casey's battered division, Couch's division, and reinforcements from Kearny. Longstreet explained the dispositions once Kearny's men joined the mix: "General Kearny, finding that he could not arrest the march, put Berry's brigade off to the swamp to flank and strike it, and took part of Jamison's brigade to follow. They got into the swamp and followed it up to the open near the Couch intrenchment, but Jenkins knew that there was some one there to meet them, and pushed his onward battle. General Hill ordered Rains's brigade to turn this new force, while Rodes attacked, but the latter's men were worn, and some of them were with the advance. Kemper's brigade was sent to support the forward battle, but General Hill directed it to his right against Berry, in front of Rains, and it seems that the heavy, swampy ground so obstructed operations on both sides as to limit their work to infantry fusillades until six o'clock."

By this time, Johnston had surmised that the Chickahominy was impassable as a result of the flooding, and he was mostly right, so he prepared to funnel Smith's men into the fight instead of having them guard the Confederate left flank, figuring the river would protect that flank. He wrote in his memoirs, "When the action began on the right, the musketry was not heard at my position on the Nine-miles road, from the unfavorable condition of the air to sound. I supposed, therefore, that the fight had not begun, and that we were hearing an artillery duel. However, a staff-officer was sent to ascertain the fact. He returned at four o'clock, with intelligence that our infantry as well as artillery had been engaged for an hour, and that our troops were pressing forward with vigor. As no approach of Federal troops from the other side of the Chickahominy had been discovered or was suspected, I hoped strongly that the bridges were impassable. It seemed to me idle, therefore, to keep General Smith longer out of action, for a contingency so remote as the coming of reenforcements from the Federal right. He was desired, therefore, to direct his division against the right flank of Longstreet's adversaries."

Johnston personally led three brigades from Whiting's division down the Nine Mile Road and into the fray on the right flank of Keyes' defenders near Fair Oaks Station (which would lend an alternative name to the entire battle itself), but unfortunately for the Confederates, the addition of most of Whiting's division was offset by the only Union reinforcements that would cross the Chickahominy that day. Once the fighting grew desperate, McClellan ordered Bull Sumner to attempt to send some reinforcements across the swollen Chickahominy, a treacherous assignment that mostly fell upon John Sedgwick's division. Israel Richardson, in command of another one of Sumner's divisions, came up to a bridge only to find that Union soldiers were waist deep in water while attempting to use it, so he was only able to get Oliver O. Howard's brigade across. Sumner proved luckier with Sedgwick's division; when met with general reluctance by Sedgwick's men at the proposition of crossing the one remaining bridge (the already damaged Grapevine Bridge), Sumner scoffed, "Impossible!? Sir, I tell you I can cross! I am ordered!" It turned out Sumner was right, but just barely, because shortly after Sedgwick's division got across, the bridge was swept away by the river.

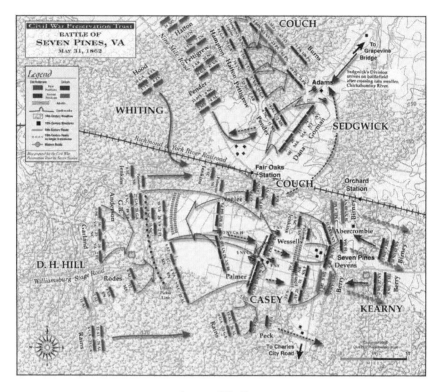

A map of the lines

As Johnston was leading men down the Nine Mile Road, he saw some of Sumner's reinforcements arriving, but he mistakenly concluded that it was only a brigade instead of an entire division and a brigade. He explained, "On my way to Longstreet's left, to combine the action of the two bodies of Confederate troops, I passed the head of General Smith's column near Fair Oaks, and saw the camp of a body of infantry of the strength of three or four regiments, apparently in the northern angle between the York River Railroad and the Nine-miles road, and the rear of a body of infantry moving in quick time from that point toward the Chickahominy, by the road to the Grape-vine Ford... I had passed the railroad some little distance with Hood's brigade, when the action commenced, and stopped to see its termination. But, being confident that the Federal troops opposing ours were those whose camps I had just seen, and therefore not more than a brigade, I did not doubt that General Smith was quite strong enough to cope with them."

As early evening was setting in, the battle had reached its fevered pitch, but both sides could not dislodge the enemy. In the fighting, Whiting's division lost three of brigade leaders, and Oliver O. Howard was seriously wounded on the Union side. Further south, on the Confederates' far right flank, more confusion reigned. Longstreet explained, "Our battle on the Williamsburg road was in a sack. We were strong enough to guard our flanks and push straight on, but the front was growing heavy. It was time for Wilcox's brigades under his last order, but nothing was heard of them. I asked General Stuart, who had joined me, if there were obstacles to Wilcox's march between the Charles City and Williamsburg roads. He reported that there was nothing more than swamp lands, hardly knee-deep. He was asked for a guide, who was sent with a courier bearing orders for them to remain with General Wilcox until he reported at my headquarters."

As darkness set in, it was apparent that the day's fighting was just about over, but it was at this point that the Confederates suffered one of the most important casualties of the Civil War. In his memoirs, Johnston described the end of the fighting that day, and how he was one of the last ones wounded in the fray:

> "This condition of affairs existed on the left at half-past 6 o'clock, and the firing on the right seemed then to be about Seven Pines. It was evident, therefore, that the battle would not be terminated that day. So I announced to my staff-officers that each regiment must sleep where it might be standing when the contest ceased for the night, to be ready to renew it at dawn next morning.

> "About seven o'clock I received a slight wound in the right shoulder from a musket-shot, and, a few moments after, was unhorsed by a heavy fragment of shell which struck my breast. Those around had me borne from the field in an ambulance; not, however, before the President, who was with General Lee, not far in the rear, had heard of the accident, and visited me, manifesting great concern, as he continued to do until I was out of danger.

> The firing ceased, terminated by darkness only, before I had been carried a mile from the field."

If anything, Johnston was understated about his injuries, which included a broken shoulder blade and a chest wound that had knocked him unconscious. Since he had to be removed from the field, G.W. Smith took over as the highest ranking officer, but aside from asserting his rank (as he had done to Longstreet earlier), he was decisive about little else. Longstreet described the Confederates' attempts to untangle themselves and prepare to renew the attack in the morning: "The brigades were so mixed up through the pines when the battle closed that there was some delay in getting the regiments to their proper commands, getting up supplies, and arranging for the morning. D. H. Hill's was put in good order and in bivouac near the Casey intrenchment; those of Longstreet between the Williamsburg road and railroad. Wilcox's brigade took position on the right, in place of the detachment under Jenkins; Pryor's brigade next on the left; Kemper, Anderson, and Colston near the stage road (Williamsburg). They made blazing fires of pine-knots to dry their clothing and blankets, and these lighted reinforcing Union troops to their lines behind the railroad."

In fairness to Smith, it might not have mattered whether he had been more aggressive, since the Union defenders were able to use the break in fighting to both strengthen their defensive line and get more men across the Chickahominy. According to Longstreet, news about the Army of the Potomac throwing up pontoon bridges unnerved Smith, and the new commander subsequently came up with an unworkable attack plan:

> "Major-General G. W. Smith was of the highest standing of the West Point classes, and, like others of the Engineers, had a big name to help him in the position to which he had been suddenly called by the incapacitation of the Confederate commander. I found his Headquarters at one o'clock in the morning, reported the work of the commands on the Williamsburg road on the 31st, and asked for part of the troops ordered up by General Johnston, that we might resume battle at daylight. He was disturbed by reports of pontoon bridges, said to be under construction for the use of other reinforcements to join the enemy from the east side, and was anxious lest the enemy might march his two corps on the east side by the upper river and occupy Richmond. But after a time these notions gave way, and he suggested that we could renew the battle on the Williamsburg road, provided we would send him one of our brigades to help hold his position and make the battle by a wheel on his right as a pivot.

> "The enemy stood: Sedgwick's division in front of Smith; Richardson's division in column of three brigades parallel to the railroad and behind it, prepared to attack my left; on Richardson's left was Birney's brigade behind the railroad, and under the enemy's third intrenched line were the balance of the Third and all of the Fourth Corps. So the plan to wheel on Smith's right as a pivot, my right stepping out on the wheel, would have left the Third and Fourth Corps to attack our rear as soon as we moved.

> "Besides, it was evident that our new commander would do nothing, and we must look to accident for such aid as might be drawn to us during the battle.

> "The plan proposed could only be considered under the hypothesis that Magruder would come in as the pivotal point, and, upon having the enemy's line fully exposed, would find the field fine for his batteries, and put them in practice without orders from his commander, and, breaking the enemy's line by an enfilade fire from his artillery, would come into battle and give it cohesive power."

Smith should've been right to be concerned about his left flank, as reconnaissance reports provided to McClellan indicated little Confederate activity in front of the Union's right. Nonetheless, McClellan didn't order a counterattack, no doubt partly out of fear that he was outnumbered.

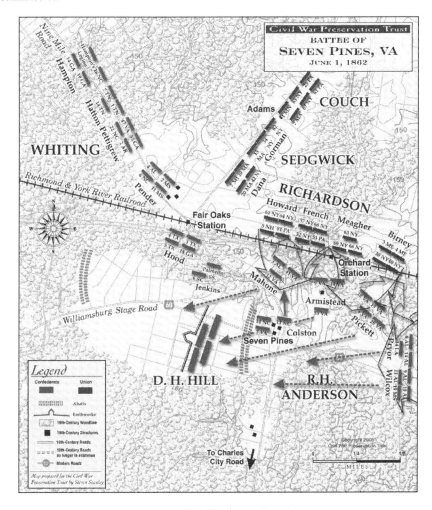

A map of the fighting on June 1

Longstreet remembered things quite differently. As the fighting recommenced that morning,

Longstreet's wing found itself in a dogged battle, but as he and Whiting pushed Smith to reinforce them, the new commander wavered. Whiting wrote back to Smith that morning, "I am going to try a diversion for Longstreet, and have found, as reported, a position for artillery. The enemy are in full view and in heavy masses. I have ordered up Lee with four pieces. The musketry firing in advance is tremendous." However, when he didn't hear from Smith, he sent back word that without orders to the contrary, he would begin withdrawing the men from the line.

Thus, as Longstreet noted, "Whiting's position, instead of being pivotal, began its rearward move at the opening fire at daybreak, and continued in that line of conduct until it reached a point of quiet. General Smith was informed that the brigade called for by him would not be sent over; that his troops were doing nothing, while all of mine were in severe battle, except a single brigade, and the enemy was massing his fighting force against me; that the grounds were so flooded that it was difficult to keep up our supply of ammunition; that with the aid of his troops the battle would be ours."

Longstreet eventually sent a dispatch back to Smith that read, ""Can you reinforce me The entire enemy seems to be opposed to me. We cannot hold out unless we get help. If we can fight together, we can finish the work to-day, and Mac's time will be up. If I cannot get help, I fear that I must fall back." By this point, however, Smith had been persuaded by other generals back at headquarters not to continue an assault. Longstreet wrote in his memoirs, "[Smith] held a council with Generals McLaws and Whiting and Chief Engineer Stevens, and submitted the question, 'Must the troops be withdrawn, or the attack continued?' All voted in favor of the former except McLaws. In a letter, since written, he has said, 'I alone urged that you be reinforced and the attack continued, and the question was reconsidered, and I was sent to learn your views.'"

As a result of the hesitation, the Confederates now found themselves in the prickly position of having to pull back in an orderly fashion during the middle of the battle. Given the relative inexperience of Civil War generals and soldiers in 1862, it's little surprise that this nearly proved disastrous for the Confederates, and a rout was staved off by just one Confederate brigade, led by George Pickett. Though he was no longer present on the field, Johnston wrote in his memoirs about Pickett's fighting: "Next morning, Brigadier-General Pickett, whose brigade was near the left of Longstreet's and Hill's line, learned that a strong body of Federal troops was before him and near. He moved forward and attacked it, driving it from that ground. Very soon, being reinforced apparently, the Federals (several brigades) assumed the offensive, and attacked him. In the mean time General Hill had sent two regiments of Colston's brigade to him. Although largely outnumbered, Pickett met this attack with great resolution, and after a brisk but short action repulsed the enemy, who disappeared, to molest him no more."

Johnston also pointed out that aside from the action in Longstreet's front that morning, there were no serious attempts by the Army of the Potomac to assault the Confederates. This was a point echoed by Longstreet as he concluded his account of the battle:

"The failure of the enemy to push the opportunity made by the precipitate retreat of General Wilcox, and Pickett's successful resistance, told that there was nothing in the reports of troops coming over from the east side to take part in the battle, and we were convinced that the river was not passable. I made an appeal for ten thousand men, that we might renew our battle without regard to General Smith and those about him. It received no more consideration than the appeal made through General McLaws.

Then General Lee, having been assigned to command, came upon the field after noon by the Nine Miles road, and, with General Smith, came over to the Williamsburg road. A similar proposition was made General Lee, but General Smith protested that the enemy was strongly fortified. At the time the enemy's main battle front was behind the railroad, fronting against me but exposed to easy enfilade fire of batteries to be posted on his right flank on the Nine Miles road, while his front against me was covered by the railway embankment. It is needless to add that under the fire of batteries so posted his lines would have been broken to confusion in twenty minutes. General Holmes marched down the Williamsburg road and rested in wait for General Lee. Like General Huger, he held rank over me. General Lee ordered the troops back to their former lines. Those on the Williamsburg road were drawn back during the night, the rear-guard, Pickett's brigade, passing the Casey works at sunrise on the 2d unmolested. Part of Richardson's division mistook the camp at Fair Oaks for the Casey camp, and claimed to have recovered it on the afternoon of the 1st, but it was not until the morning of the 2d that the Casey camp was abandoned.

The Confederate losses in the two days fight were 6134; the Union losses, 5031."

Given his lackluster performance on the night of June 30 and the morning of June 1, not to mention the serious challenges facing the Confederates, it should perhaps come as little surprise that Smith's command of the Army of Northern Virginia had officially lasted less than 18 hours. Longstreet sarcastically wrote about Smith's career after being removed from command: "He reported sick on the 2d and left the army. When ready for duty he was assigned about Richmond and the seaboard of North Carolina. He applied to be restored to command of his division in the field, but the authorities thought his services could be used better elsewhere. He resigned his commission in the Confederate service, went to Georgia, and joined Joe Brown's militia, where he found congenial service, better suited to his ideas of vigorous warfare."

Chapter 5: The Aftermath of the Battle

From his first day in command, Lee faced a daunting, seemingly impossible challenge. McClellan had maneuvered nearly 100,000 troops to within seven miles of Richmond, three Union units were closing in on General Jackson's Confederates in Virginia's Shenandoah Valley, and a fourth Union army was camped on the Rappahannock River ostensibly ready to come to McClellan's aid.

Moreover, as Longstreet indicated in his memoirs, Lee had a mixed record by this time in the war and was not beloved by the Army of Northern Virginia: "The assignment of General Lee to command the army of Northern Virginia was far from reconciling the troops to the loss of our beloved chief, Joseph E. Johnston, with whom the army had been closely connected since its earliest active life. All hearts had learned to lean upon him with confidence, and to love him dearly. General Lee's experience in active field work was limited to his West Virginia campaign against General Rosecrans, which was not successful. His services on our coast defences were known as able, and those who knew him in Mexico as one of the principal engineers of General Scott's column, marching for the capture of the capital of that great republic, knew that as military engineer he was especially distinguished; but officers of the line are not apt to look to the staff in choosing leaders of soldiers, either in tactics or strategy. There were, therefore, some misgivings as to the power and skill for field service of the new commander. The change was accepted, however, as a happy relief from the existing halting policy of the late temporary commander."

Of course, Lee would quickly demonstrate he was the opposite of indecisive. With Stonewall Jackson having bottled up the Union in the Shenandoah Valley, Lee wrote to him on June 11, "Your recent successes have been the cause of the liveliest joy in this army as well as in the country. The admiration excited by your skill and boldness has been constantly mingled with solicitude for your situation. The practicability of reinforcing you has been the subject of earnest consideration. It has been determined to do so at the expense of weakening this army. Brigadier-General Lawton, with six regiments from Georgia, is on the way to you, and Brigadier-General Whiting, with eight veteran regiments, leaves here to-day. The object is to enable you to crush the forces opposed to you. Leave your enfeebled troops to watch the country and guard the passes covered by your cavalry and artillery, and with your main body, including Ewell's division and Lawton's and Whiting's commands, move rapidly to Ashland by rail or otherwise, as you may find most advantageous, and sweep down between the Chickahominy and Pamunkey, cutting up the enemy's communications, etc., while this army attacks General McClellan in front. He will thus, I think, be forced to come out of his intrenchments, where he is strongly posted on the Chickahominy, and apparently preparing to move by gradual approaches on Richmond. Keep me advised of your movements, and, if practicable, precede your troops, that we may confer and arrange for simultaneous attack."

Jackson

On June 12, as McClellan sat on Richmond's eastern outskirts waiting for reinforcements, Lee began to ring the city with troop entrenchments. Realizing that McClellan's flank appeared to be exposed and hoping to hit it with Jackson's army, Lee tasked J.E.B. Stuart with assessing whether the Union army had any real protection north and west of the exposed flank. Stuart suggested that his men circumnavigate McClellan's army, to which Lee responded with deference that would become his trademark and a symbol of his trust in his subordinates. Lee gave Stuart vague orders: "You will return as soon as the object of your expedition is accomplished, and you must bear constantly in mind, while endeavoring to execute the general purpose of your mission, not to hazard unnecessarily your command or to attempt what your judgment may not approve; but be content to accomplish all the good you can without feeling it necessary to obtain all that might be desired. I recommend that you take only such men as can stand the expedition, and that you take every means in your power to save and cherish those you take. You must leave sufficient cavalry here for the service of this army, and remember that one of the chief objects of your expedition is to gain intelligence for the guidance of future operations."

Lee

Stuart

With that, Stuart embarked with 1200 troopers on a spectacular three-day, 150 mile ride in the rear of and around the entire Army of the Potomac, a mission that would require him to keep just ahead of pursuing horsemen led by Union Brig. General Philip St. George Cooke, Stuart's father-in-law. Though daunting and dangerous, Stuart and his men successfully completed the historic ride, with Stuart returning to Richmond to report to Lee on June 14 and most of his cavalry returning the following day. Stuart was able not only to report that McClellan's flank was indeed completely unguarded, he delivered 165 captured Union soldiers, 260 horses and mules, and a collection of quartermaster and ordinance supplies as well. The "ride around McClellan" proved to be a public relations sensation for Stuart, resulting in dramatic newspaper accounts, hordes of women cheering and strewing flower petals in his path when he rode through the streets of Richmond, and his face appearing on the front pages of most newspapers in both the North and South. The flamboyant officer relished every second of his ride, later writing, "There was something of the sublime in the implicit confidence and unquestioning trust of the rank and file in a leader guiding them straight, apparently, into the very jaws of the enemy, every step appearing to them to diminish the faintest hope of extrication."

Although the Battle of Seven Pines was tactically inconclusive, McClellan's resolve to keep pushing forward seemed to all but vanish. He confided in a letter to his wife, "I am tired of the sickening sight of the battlefield, with its mangled corpses & poor suffering wounded! Victory has no charms for me when purchased at such cost."

McClellan maneuvered his army so that it was all south of the Chickahominy, but as he settled in for an expected siege, Lee went about preparing Richmond's defenses and devising his own aggressive attacks. With more Confederate troops swelling the ranks, Lee's army was McClellan's equal by late June, and on June 25, Lee commenced an all-out attempt to destroy McClellan's army in a series of fierce battles known as the Seven Days Battles.

After a stalemate in the first fighting at Oak Grove, Lee's army kept pushing ahead, using Stonewall Jackson to attack McClellan's right. Although Stonewall Jackson was unusually lethargic during the week's fighting, the appearance of his "foot cavalry" spooked McClellan even more, and McClellan was now certain he was opposed by 200,000 men, more than double the actual size of Lee's army. It also made McClellan think that the Confederates were threatening his supply line, forcing him to shift his army toward the James River to draw supplies.

On June 26, the Union defenders sharply repulsed the Confederate attacks at Mechanicsville, in part due to the fact that Stonewall Jackson had his troops bivouac for the night despite the fact heavy gunfire indicating a large battle was popping off within earshot. When the Confederates had more success the next day at Gaines' Mills, McClellan continued his strategic retreat, maneuvering his army toward a defensive position on the James River and all but abandoning the siege.

McClellan managed to keep his forces in tact, ultimately retreating to Harrison's Landing on the James River and establishing a new base of operation. Feeling increasingly at odds with his superiors, in a letter sent from Gaines' Mills, Virginia dated June 28, 1862, a frustrated McClellan wrote to Secretary of War Stanton, "If I save the army now, I tell you plainly that I owe no thanks to any other person in the Washington. You have done your best to sacrifice this army." McClellan's argument, however, flies in the face of common knowledge that he had become so obsessed with having sufficient supplies that he'd actually moved to Gaines' Mill to accommodate the massive amount of provisions he'd accumulated. Ultimately unable to move his cache of supplies as quickly as his men were needed, McClellan eventually ran railroad cars full of food and supplies into the Pamunkey River rather than leave them behind for the Confederates.

Despite the fact all of Lee's battle plans had been poorly executed by his generals, particularly Stonewall Jackson, he ordered one final assault against McClellan's army at Malvern Hill. Incredibly, McClellan was not even on the field for that battle, having left via steamboat back to Harrison's Landing. Biographer Ethan Rafuse notes McClellan's absence from the battlefield was inexcusable, literally leaving the Army of the Potomac leaderless during pitched battle, but McClellan often behaved coolly under fire, so it is likely not a question of McClellan's personal courage.

Ironically, Malvern Hill was one of the Union army's biggest successes during the Peninsula Campaign. Union artillery had silenced its Confederate counterparts, but Lee still ordered an infantry attack by D.H. Hill's division, which never got within 100 yards of the Union line. After the war, Hill famously said of Malvern Hill, "It wasn't war. It was murder." Later that evening, General Isaac Trimble, best known for leading a division during Pickett's Charge at Gettysburg, began moving his troops forward as if to attack, only to be stopped by Stonewall Jackson, who asked "What are you going to do?" When Trimble replied that he was going to charge, Jackson countered, "General Hill has just tried with his entire division and been repulsed. I guess you'd better not try it."

After Malvern Hill, McClellan withdrew his army to Harrison's Landing, where it was protected by the Union Navy along the James River and had its flanks secured by the river itself. At this point, the bureaucratic bickering between McClellan and Washington started flaring up again, as McClellan refused to recommence an advance without reinforcements. After weeks of indecision, the Army of the Potomac was finally ordered to evacuate the Peninsula and link up with John Pope's army in northern Virginia, as the administration was more comfortable having their forces fighting on one line instead of exterior lines.

Making things all the worse, McClellan's delays had allowed Lee to swing his army into Northern Virginia and decisively defeat Pope's army at Second Bull Run in late August before the vast majority of McClellan's army could arrive as reinforcements. In fact, only one of McClellan's corps, Porter's V Corps, would reach Manassas to participate in that battle, and upon his arrival in Washington, McClellan told reporters that his failure to defeat Lee in Virginia was due to Lincoln not sending sufficient reinforcements.

Online Resources

Other books about the Civil War by Charles River Editors

Other books about the Peninsula Campaign on Amazon

Bibliography

Downs, Alan C. "Fair Oaks/Seven Pines." In Encyclopedia of the American Civil War: A Political, Social, and Military History, edited by David S. Heidler and Jeanne T. Heidler. New York: W. W. Norton & Company, 2000. ISBN 0-393-04758-X.

Eicher, David J. The Longest Night: A Military History of the Civil War. New York: Simon & Schuster, 2001. ISBN 0-684-84944-5.

Esposito, Vincent J. West Point Atlas of American Wars. New York: Frederick A. Praeger, 1959. OCLC 5890637. The collection of maps (without explanatory text) is available online at the West Point website.

Lowe, Thaddeus S. C. My Balloons in Peace and War: Memoirs of Thaddeus S.C. Lowe, Chief of the Aeronautic Corps of the Army of the United States during the Civil War. Lewiston, NY: Edwin Mellen Press, 2004. ISBN 978-0-7734-6522-0.

Miller, William J. The Battles for Richmond, 1862. National Park Service Civil War Series. Fort Washington, PA: U.S. National Park Service and Eastern National, 1996. ISBN 0-915992-93-0.

Salmon, John S. The Official Virginia Civil War Battlefield Guide. Mechanicsburg, PA: Stackpole Books, 2001. ISBN 0-8117-2868-4.

Sears, Stephen W. To the Gates of Richmond: The Peninsula Campaign. New York: Ticknor and Fields, 1992. ISBN 0-89919-790-6.

Made in the USA
Middletown, DE
24 November 2020